The history of Boy Scouting, from its rather unusual beginnings, through its rapid development into a still-growing international organization, is here to be enjoyed by all Scouts, would-be Scouts, and their friends.

Included in this account are exciting true stories of life-saving and other rescue work for which Boy Scouts earned the National Court of Honor medal for heroism. Here, too, is the story of a teenaged Peruvian Scout who undertook and completed probably the longest "hike" in the history of Scouting—more than 10,000 miles. Another exciting account is that of Paul Siple, an Eagle Scout from Pennsylvania, who accompanied Commander Richard Byrd on his 1928 expedition to the South Pole.

The pleasures of camping, the rollicking fun and forming of worldwide friendships at jamborees, and the selfless work on conservation and other community projects— all are part of the spirit of Scouting, and all are here in this comprehensive picture of this growing organization.

Story
of the
Boy Scouts

BY WYATT BLASSINGAME

ILLUSTRATED BY DAVID HODGES

GARRARD PUBLISHING COMPANY
CHAMPAIGN, ILLINOIS

Picture credits:

Acme Photo: p. 75

Authenticated News International: p. 83, 90

Baden-Powell: The Two Lives of a Hero by William Hillcourt (New York: G. P. Putnam's Sons, 1964): p. 20

Boy Scouts of America, New Brunswick, New Jersey: p. 22, 29, 31, 34, 35, 36, 46 (bottom), 66, 94

Walter MacPeek: p. 2, 46 (top right), 57

Wide World Photos: p. 9, 46 (top left), 86, 92

Contents

1. Philmont Adventure

The ranger at the Philmont Scout Ranch in New Mexico was young, tall, and lean. Only two years earlier he had been an Explorer himself. Now, standing beside the campfire, he was advising the newly arrived group of boys.

"I only go this far on the hike with you," he told them. "Tomorrow I go back to headquarters. You Scouts and your leader will be on your own for the big hike across the ranch."

He paused, and the boys sitting around the campfire waited. It was dark now, so quiet they could hear the whisper of wind in the piñon needles. Somewhere an owl hooted. Off to the west, where the mountains rose sharply, an animal made a long wailing noise.

Young Joe Lurton whispered, "A mountain lion!"

The ranger grinned. "No, a coyote. It won't bother you. Neither will a mountain lion. You might see a mountain lion on this hike, but the odds are against it. A mountain lion is as afraid of you as you are of it."

"I doubt that," one of the boys said. "You don't know how scared I am of mountain lions."

Everyone laughed. It was a good sound there in the glow of the campfire.

"What you Scouts do need to remember," the ranger said, "are the bears. They won't bother you unless you bother them. But . . . ."

"Then there's no need to worry," the same boy said. "Because I'm sure not going to bother them."

"Unless you are careful," the ranger said,

American Boy Scouts hike the many trails of
the 127,000 acre Philmont Scout Ranch.

"the bears will bother your food, whether you bother them or not. So remember to hang your food well off the ground and between two trees. If you just hang it in a tree, the bear may climb the tree and get it."

He went on to tell the Scouts something about the Philmont Scout Ranch. "As you know," he said, "the nearest town is Cimarron, New Mexico. In Spanish 'Cimarron' means 'wild' or 'untamed.' This is a wild, untamed country. The ranch contains more than 200 square miles, most of it wilderness. This is the same country where Kit Carson, Joe Meek, and other mountain men trapped beaver and fought Indians. It hasn't changed much. There are places where you can still see the wagon ruts of the old Santa Fe Trail. Before you return to headquarters from your hike, you'll have a chance to go exploring on horseback. You will be able to hunt with bows and arrows. You can even pan gold."

The surrounding darkness seemed to push closer to the campfire now. The tents, put up earlier, were barely visible. A little nervously the boys said good night to one another, to the ranger, to their Scout leader, and went to bed.

Snug in his sleeping bag, Joe Lurton lay looking up into the darkness. He was tired, but he did not want to go to sleep. Not yet. He was still too excited about what had happened to him in the last few days and what might happen in the next week.

Joe's home, and that of all the boys in his outfit, was in Florida. The highest "hill" in Joe's town was a sand dune about ten feet above the Gulf of Mexico. Now there were mountains all around him, some of them so high that clouds hid their tops. At home in the middle of summer, he would have slept with an air conditioner to keep him cool. Here in July cold air flowed down from the mountains like a river, and he snuggled deep in his sleeping bag to keep warm.

He was almost asleep. Suddenly someone was shouting, "Bears! Bears!" Joe almost shot

from his sleeping bag. He scrambled out of his tent, with Gregg Diamont, his tent mate, right behind him. Around them flashlights were glittering like fireflies. One boy was shouting, "I heard them! Over where we hung the food!"

The ranger and Doc Thompson, the Scout leader, were standing between the trees where the food was hung. Their flashlights pointed at the ground. Joe could see the big claw-tipped tracks.

"A bear all right," the ranger said. "Now you fellows see why it is necessary to hang your food in a safe place. Otherwise you would have a long, hungry hike ahead of you."

Gradually the boys quieted down again. Joe and Gregg went back to their tent. But still Joe could not sleep. He was thinking of bears and of the long ride from Florida on the chartered bus, with all the boys singing as they rode. He thought of the nights they had spent at army bases on the way and of the visit to Carlsbad Caverns and to the Alamo.

Ahead of them now lay miles of western wilderness, crisscrossed with trails. And along all these trails were other boys, from New York and Illinois, from California and Alaska.

"Gregg?" Joe whispered. "Are you awake?"

"Yes."

"What are you thinking?"

"About tomorrow, I guess. But it's all sort of mixed up. I was thinking about last summer too, when I went to the Scout Canoe Base up in northern Minnesota. It's the one called the Charles Sommers Wilderness Canoe Base. For a week we lived in the woods and went paddling down rivers and across lakes along the Canadian border. I didn't think then that I'd ever have as much fun again in my life."

"Maybe I can go there next summer," Joe said. "Or to the Scout Canoe Base in Wisconsin, called the Boulder Junction Base."

"I know. That's what I was thinking. About all the Scouts here at Philmont and at the canoe bases. And about other Scouts going down into the Grand Canyon, or climbing mountains and having fun and adventure. Not only in this country but in England, in Japan, and all over the world. I guess I was sort of wondering how it all began."

2. Baden-Powell, Army Scout

The year was 1881. A young lieutenant named Robert Stephenson Baden-Powell was on duty with the British Army in India. In the middle of the night, he awoke to hear the wild whine of the wind. He heard his tent shudder and strain at the guy lines. Suddenly outside his tent men began to shout in alarm.

Baden-Powell leaped to his feet. In the cold darkness he jerked on his clothing and buckled his revolver around his waist. It was just the sort of night the natives would choose for an attack, he thought as he ran outside.

Against the darkness lanterns waved crazily. A sergeant came running past. "What's happening?" Baden-Powell called.

"There's no attack, sir. But half our tents have blown away in the storm. You are lucky yours didn't."

The Lieutenant grinned. "That's not luck. I made sure it was put up properly."

"Yes, sir. But those that did blow away frightened the horses. They stampeded. Nearly all of them are gone. We may have trouble rounding them up."

By morning the storm had blown itself out. By noon all the horses had been recaptured—except one. The best horse in the regiment, the Colonel's favorite, had disappeared. Young Lieutenant Baden-Powell asked the Colonel's permission to go look for it. "I think I can track it, sir."

"Track it?" The Colonel frowned. American Indians were supposed to be able to track ani-

mals, but not British army officers. On the other hand, there was nothing to lose. "Go ahead," he said.

Riding his own horse, Baden-Powell went a short distance out of camp. Then slowly he began to circle the camp. His blue eyes searched the ground carefully.

Ever since he was a small boy, B-P, as his friends called him, had been interested in studying nature. He had taught himself to follow the tracks of wild animals to see how they lived. It paid off, for now he found the tracks of the Colonel's horse. They were headed toward the mountains, and B-P followed.

This was dangerous going. Great Britain was fighting a people called Afghans in northern India. Many of the Afghan troops were hidden in the mountains. They would welcome the chance to kill a lone British officer. Carefully Baden-Powell studied the rocks and bushes ahead of him.

He found no enemies, but he soon found the Colonel's horse and brought it back to camp.

18

The incident seemed unimportant at the time. B-P thought little of it. But it brought the young officer to the Colonel's attention. After this when a man was needed to scout the enemy position, B-P was selected. The more scouting he did, the better he became at it. He learned how important scouting was to an army and how little the average British soldier knew about it. B-P began to train the men serving under him.

Years later when Baden-Powell had become a 41-year-old colonel, he wrote a small book about his training methods. It was called *Aids to Scouting*. Like the incident of the lost horse, B-P did not think much about it. Yet what he had done would change the lives of men and boys all over the world.

B-P was in South Africa in 1900, the year the book was published. Great Britain was then at war with the Boers, the white settlers who controlled South Africa. At a place called Mafeking, B-P, with fewer than 2,000 men, was cut off from the rest of the British Army.

B-P made this sketch during the long Boer siege at Mafeking.

His group was surrounded by many thousands of the enemy. Day after day, week after week, he and his men held out. All the scouting skills B-P had learned were used to confuse the enemy and keep them off balance.

The weeks dragged into months. The British were running out of food and ammunition. B-P ordered the horses killed, one by one, for food. Even the bones and skin were boiled to make soup. The shoes of the horses were melted to make bullets.

The siege of Mafeking lasted for 217 days. Finally a unit of the British Army came to the rescue.

When the war was over, B-P went back to England. Now he was a great national hero. Queen Victoria sent him a message of congratulation. He was made a major general, the youngest general in the British Army. Everywhere he went, crowds gathered to cheer him.

Boys in particular admired Baden-Powell. All over the country they began to read the book he had written, *Aids to Scouting*. They began to go into the fields and woods to practice the things he had described. Many of them wrote to ask questions about scouting. Carefully, B-P answered each letter.

3. Woodcraft Indians and the Sons of Daniel Boone

While English boys were reading B-P's book *Aids to Scouting*, a man named Ernest Thompson Seton was buying a farm in Connecticut. History was later to make a strange connection between these two events.

Seton was an artist and writer and also an outdoorsman. The books he wrote and the pictures he drew described wild animals and life in the Far West. Now he planned to use his

Connecticut farm for experiments in conservation of plants and wildlife. As part of his program he put a high fence around the farm.

Suddenly there was trouble where Seton least expected it. The boys in the neighborhood did not understand what he was doing. All they knew was that he had fenced in land where they had hunted and fished.

So they declared war. They painted dirty words on his gate. They cut his fence. They set fires in his woods.

Seton tried to talk with the boys, but they were too angry to listen. They cut more holes in his fence and set more fires.

"Call the police," some of Seton's friends said. "Have the boys put in jail. That's the only way to handle this." But it did not seem the right way to Ernest Seton. He could remember how he had felt when he was a boy.

One day he had an idea. He went to the school and asked the principal if he would call together all the boys who were fourteen or older.

Slowly the boys came into the room. They expected an angry lecture. Instead, Seton invited them all to come to his farm on Friday afternoon.

"Bring a couple of blankets," he said. "That's all you'll need. I'll have everything else ready. You can swim in the lake, have supper around a campfire, and camp out like Indians for the weekend."

The boys listened, wondering if this were some kind of trick. Not one boy promised to come to the farm. But no boy said he wouldn't.

Seton thought perhaps ten or twelve boys might accept his invitation. But by the middle of Friday afternoon not one single boy had shown up. Seton kept waiting.

At last they came, 41 of them. They kept close together, not sure of what they were getting into. Quietly they followed Seton to the logs he had ready for the campfire. Wide-eyed they looked at the Indian tepees he had built. Finally one boy asked, "May we go swimming?"

"Sure," Seton said. "And make some noise

when you do it. It's not right for boys to be
this quiet."

They realized he meant it. Howling like Indians, they stripped off their clothes and raced
for the lake. They rowed boats and fished and
dived from tree limbs. In one meal they ate
all the food he had bought for the weekend.
That was all right with Seton, and quickly he

sent to town for more. Finally, tired and well fed, the boys gathered around the campfire.

Seton began to tell them stories about his life among cowboys and Indians. He told them about the hunt for the giant wolf, Lobo, who was so smart no one could trap or poison him. He told them about the chase of a wild mustang called the Black Pacer. The mustang never galloped, he only paced; yet he was so fast and so powerful that not even a team of men riding one horse after another could run him down. He told them about the tricks that Indians used in buffalo hunting.

Finally he asked, "Say, fellows, how should we set up this camp? Do you want to do it any old way or do it real Indian fashion?"

The boys shouted together, "Indian fashion!"

"All right," Seton told them. "You'll have to elect a chief, then make rules for the tribe."

It was a wonderful weekend. But the fun did not end with that Sunday night. Week after week the boys came back to Seton's farm. They learned woodcraft and the ways of the

Indians. They came to know all the birds and animals, how the crows taught their young, and the cunning of foxes.

No longer did the boys cut holes in Seton's fence or set fire to his woods. When they left a campfire, they put it out and cleaned around it so well no one could tell they had been there.

In some of his magazine articles, Ernest Thompson Seton wrote about his Woodcraft Indians, as he called them. He told how other boys could form similar groups. Soon bands of Woodcraft Indians began to be formed all over the United States.

Ernest Thompson Seton was not the only American working at this time to bring boys and the outdoors together. Another was Daniel Carter Beard.

Like Seton, Dan Beard was both an artist and a writer. He had spent most of his life outdoors, and he looked it. He was a small, lean man with a leathery, wrinkled face and twinkling eyes that looked as if he were just about to tell a funny joke. But about boys and the outdoors he was very serious. In 1905 he wrote a magazine article addressed to boys all over the country. In it he said:

"I propose that we form a society to be called 'The Sons of Daniel Boone.' Both American and Canadian boys will unite in one brotherhood to protect our brothers in fur, feathers, scales, and bark.

"Our object will be: the study of woodcraft; outdoor sports, and fun; along with serious work to save and protect our native wild plants, birds, and beasts.

". . . we will call each branch of the club a 'fort.' Each fort will be named for a famous American who loved the outdoors. . . .

"The leader of each fort will be called 'Dan Boone' instead of 'president.' The secretary will be 'Davy Crockett,' the treasurer will be 'Kit Carson.'

"Each fort must have an old unloaded gun for a Tally Gun. It need not work. It need only have a stock and barrel. The pioneers

28

Old Dan Beard tells two young Scouts about the early days of Sons of Daniel Boone.

kept records by notches cut in the stock of their guns. The forts will keep records of their good deeds in protecting forests and wildlife by cutting notches in their gun stocks."

Dan Beard got famous generals and admirals and naturalists to help with his boys' clubs. He got Buffalo Bill to help. He even got President Theodore Roosevelt. All these men were anxious to bring American boys and the outdoors together. Soon the Sons of Daniel Boone became the biggest boys' club in America. All over the country boys were chanting:

Cut a notch, cut a notch, cut a notch soon,
For we are the Sons of Daniel Boone!

In many ways the Sons of Daniel Boone and the Woodcraft Indians were alike. There were also some smaller clubs for boys interested in woodcraft and conservation. But they had no close connection with one another. Nor was there any tie between these boys in America and those in England who were writing to Baden-Powell about scouting. That tie would come in a very strange way.

4. The Boy Scouts Are Formed

The largest club for boys in England was called the Boys' Brigade. It was a military type of club founded by William Smith. The boys drilled like soldiers. When General Baden-Powell returned as a hero from South Africa, he was asked to review a Boys' Brigade parade. Afterward B-P praised Mr. Smith for "doing a wonderful work."

"But I think it would be more fun if the boys had other things to do besides drill," he added. "Why don't you teach them scouting?"

"Why don't *you* teach them?" Mr. Smith asked. "Many of them have read your *Aids to Scouting*. Some of them know it by heart."

The General frowned. "I wrote that book for soldiers, for men at war."

"Then write one for boys at peace."

"I just don't have time." This was true. Besides doing his job with the army, B-P was responding to lecture invitations from all over England.

Even so, he could not stop thinking how important it was that boys learn scouting. This would be scouting for peace, not war, he thought. It would help boys grow strong and alert. It would teach them the value of preserving the woods and streams and natural resources of the nation. Working with boys to promote peace and conservation, he thought, could be an even more important service to his country than being a general in the army.

The more Baden-Powell thought about this idea, the more important it seemed. He began to make notes on how such a club or group of clubs could be formed. He noted the kind of uniform the boys could wear and the club laws they could have.

Then one day he received a book by Ernest Thompson Seton called *The Birch-bark Roll of Woodcraft Indians.* In it Seton told about how American boys formed "gangs" of Woodcraft Indians, about the games they played, and about the Indian lore they practiced.

B-P was very much impressed. He wrote to Seton: "It may interest you to know that I had been drawing up a scheme with a handbook to it, for the education of boys as scouts —which curiously runs much on the line of yours. So I need scarcely say your work has a very special interest for me."

Later, when Seton visited England, the two men met. Both were writers and artists. Both were outdoorsmen. And both had a great interest in boys. Almost at once they became good friends.

The two men met only once before Seton went back to America. But now the idea for a club that would teach boys about scouting was taking final shape in B-P's mind. To try out this idea, he decided to take a group of boys camping.

The place B-P chose was a wooded island called Brownsea, just off the coast of England. The boys he selected were a mixed lot indeed. Some were rich, some were poor; some were educated, some were not; some had traveled all over the world, some had never been away from home. It was B-P's purpose to see how

B-P and his guests plan a game at the first Boy Scout camp at Brownsea Island in 1907.

These boys root for their team as B-P and some visitors to Brownsea look on.

such different boys would get along, living closely together in camp.

The boys did not know the purpose of the camp, and they did not care. They knew they were going with General Baden-Powell, the hero of Mafeking, and that was enough.

They arrived at Brownsea on July 29, 1907, and stayed until August 9. They learned to track animals and to signal to one another across the lake. They learned to pitch tents and to build fires and cook outdoors. They all got along well together and had the time of

This drawing by B-P was an illustration in *Scouting for Boys.*

their lives. It was, though none of them knew it, the first Boy Scout camp in history.

B-P left Brownsea more convinced than ever of the importance of scouting. He took time from his other work to write a book called *Scouting for Boys.* He told how boys could learn scoutcraft on their own, how they could go into the woods to practice scouting, and how they could form patrols for themselves.

At first B-P thought scouting would be a

part-time activity of groups such as the Boys' Brigade. But throughout England boys wanted to be scouts and nothing else. By the hundreds, and then by the thousands, they formed their own patrols. Some of them had men for scoutmasters; some had no leaders at all. They wrote to B-P for advice and to the scouting magazine he had started. The letters came in a flood.

Finally B-P resigned from the army so he could give his full time to this new and amazing "army" of boys that was now called the Boy Scouts.

All this happened in England, where many boys were attracted to Scouting because of the fame of General Baden-Powell. In the United States most boys had never heard of the General or of the Boy Scouts either. American boys belonged to the Sons of Daniel Boone, the Woodcraft Indians, and other groups. Yet all these groups were destined to become Boy Scouts. The story starts with one foggy night in London, England.

5. How Scouting Came to America

It was late autumn, 1909. In London the fog was so thick that lighted windows could be seen only a few feet away. Street corners vanished in the gloom. Buildings seemed to waver with the mist, barely visible one moment, gone the next. William D. Boyce, an American newspaper publisher, was completely lost. He stood staring into the fog, trying to decide what to do next.

"May I help you, sir?"

Boyce turned to look at the person who had spoken. It was a boy; he could see that much.

"I'm trying to find my hotel," Boyce said. "But I don't know which way to go."

"What is the name of the hotel?"

Boyce told him. "This way," the boy said. Together they moved off through the fog. "You're a stranger in London, sir?"

"I'm an American."

"I thought so, by your accent. Here's your hotel. You were close to it already."

"Thank you," Boyce said. He took a shilling from his pocket and held it toward the boy.

"No, thank you," the boy said. "I don't want pay for doing a good deed. I'm a Boy Scout."

"Boy Scout?" Mr. Boyce said. "What's that?"

"One of General Baden-Powell's Boy Scouts, sir. You must know about the General."

"I know about the hero of Mafeking," Boyce said. "But I never heard of Boy Scouts."

The boy told him. His voice was so eager, so excited, that William Boyce, sitting in his hotel room later, kept thinking about what he had heard. Next day he called on General Baden-Powell. He told the General about the boy who had helped him find his way through the fog. "I don't know who he was," Boyce said. "He never told me his name. But he certainly interested me in this Boy Scout movement of yours."

Baden-Powell told Boyce of the patrols being formed all over England and how excited the boys were about Scouting. The General was as excited as the boys. And very soon William Boyce was as excited as the General.

When Boyce went back to the United States,

he took with him a trunk full of information about Scouting. Soon he had friends and businessmen interested in such a movement. He went to Washington to talk with government officials. There he officially registered a new corporation.

Its name was Boy Scouts of America. The date was February 8, 1910.

At first the Boy Scout movement in the United States was a sort of hit-or-miss organization. Mr. Boyce was busy with his own work and had little time to give to Scouting. Many boys heard about the movement and were eager to join, but they did not know how to go about it. Some of them wrote to their YMCA's for help.

One of the YMCA officials was a man named Edgar Robinson. He began to get letters from boys all over the country. They asked: "What are the Boy Scouts? How can I join?" The YMCA could not help them, so Mr. Robinson went to call on William Boyce.

"The Boy Scouts need a good central organization," Boyce said. "But I don't have the time to give to it. What we really need is a lot of important people to help."

"I'll see if I can line up some leadership," Robinson said.

He called a meeting of men he knew were interested in helping boys. Among them were some of the most important men in the country. There were newspaper and magazine publishers, teachers and businessmen.

There were also Ernest Thompson Seton, who had started the Woodcraft Indians, and Dan Beard, who headed the Sons of Daniel Boone. Each of these men was, naturally, very much interested in his own group. But they both knew that it would be best for the boys to have one truly strong, nationwide organization. So without hesitation Seton and Beard agreed to merge their groups with the Boy Scouts. In the new organization Seton was named Chief Scout. Dan Beard was one of three National Commissioners.

Seton and Beard had other jobs to do, and

so did everyone else at the meeting. These men could volunteer only part of their time. Yet they knew that, to organize the new movement properly, a full-time leader of great ability was needed. William Boyce and several other wealthy men donated money to hire a man named James E. West.

Jimmy West did not look like a man to lead Boy Scouts. He was a cripple. He no longer used crutches, but he walked with a limp. He was in pain much of the time. But Jimmy West had learned to ignore pain in order to accomplish the things he set out to do.

Jimmy West had been raised in an orphans' home. Small, sickly, he had been forced to work with the girls in the sewing room rather than with the boys outdoors. But he worked without complaining.

This was in the 1890's when most boys left the orphanage to take regular jobs by the time they were sixteen. Jimmy West said he wanted to go to high school. To earn his way, he had to get up before daylight one day a week to work in the orphanage laundry. He had to do more work in the afternoons and study late at night. But he finished high school. Then, to the amazement of everyone, he said he was going to college.

He needed more money than he could make in the laundry. He asked for a job in a bicycle shop. The owner looked at Jimmy's crutches and shook his head. "I need help," he said. "But I need someone who can ride a bicycle."

"If I learn to ride, may I have the job?"

"Yes."

"May I borrow a bicycle?"

"Take that old one over there," the man said. "Yon can't do much harm to it."

When Jimmy West came back to the bicycle shop, his clothing was torn, his arm was skinned, and his nose was bloody. But he could ride a bicycle, and he got the job.

Jimmy West went to college. He went on to become a lawyer. Because he liked boys and understood what it was to be poor, he worked to pass laws that would help poor chil-

dren. Once President Theodore Roosevelt told him, "You are one of those patriotic citizens to whom this country owes a peculiar debt of gratitude."

This was the man who became the first Chief Scout Executive of the Boy Scouts of America. Under his leadership Boy Scout troops were formed all over the United States. Important men volunteered to be Scoutmasters.

As the movement grew, gradual changes took place in the organization. Cub scouting was added for the younger boys. Explorer, Sea, and Air Scouting were added for the older boys. From the day of January 2, 1911, when James E. West took over, the Boy Scouts of America continued to grow.

Years later some people would argue over who started the Boy Scouts. Was it Baden-Powell? Dan Beard or Ernest Seton? William Boyce or Edgar Robinson or James West?

To all these men the question was unimportant. Each one of them gave the same answer. "It doesn't matter who started the Scouts," they said. "What matters is the boys themselves and what is best for them."

Once when Baden-Powell was visiting America, he said: "I am sometimes called 'The Father of Scouting.' But the truth is, I am one of its many, many uncles."

When Boy Scouts go camping they try their hand at cooking, plan a day's activities, and test their other camping skills.

6.   Court of Honor

Heavy snows had fallen during the winter. In the spring the rain fell day after day. The soaked earth could not absorb the water. Little trickles ran from fields and roads into ditches. Ditches turned into small brooks. Brooks became rivers. Everywhere the water rose higher. Then, almost suddenly, it overflowed the banks. A great muddy flood roared across much of Ohio and Indiana, sweeping away bridges, roads, and houses.

This was the spring of 1913. Scouting was still new in America. All over the country boys were busily forming new troops, but often they had no real Scoutmasters. Some adults had never even heard of Scouting, and many paid little attention to what they did hear. Scouting, they thought, was some kind of game for boys; it was nothing important.

But when the floods took over much of Ohio and Indiana, Boy Scouts turned out, by ones and twos, by patrols and troops, to help fight it. Scouts stood waist-deep in the swirling water to help old people and young children stagger to safety. They filled sandbags and carried them into place to hold back the water. They formed living chains to rescue furniture from houses about to be swept away.

One story of a Scout's heroism was told by a farmer. The farmer had been away from home. When he returned, he found his way blocked by deep, rushing water. Across the water he could see his house, with the flood rising rapidly around it. He could see his wife standing on the porch, holding their twin babies in her arms. But when he tried to reach the house, the flood swept him off his feet. He had to fight his way back to the road.

Frantically the farmer looked for a boat of some kind. There was no boat. But a boy was suddenly there. The farmer did not know where the boy came from or who he was. The boy did not volunteer his name. He merely said he was a Boy Scout.

With rope from the farmer's wagon, the

Scout lashed several logs together to form a raft. He and the farmer poled the raft to the house. They rescued the farmer's wife and children and brought them back to safety. After that the Scout disappeared, as unknown as the English Scout who had once helped William Boyce find his way through a London fog.

One of the cities most damaged by this flood was Portsmouth, Ohio. Later the editor of the local paper wrote:

"The flood has come and gone. The loss has been heavy, destruction great, but . . . the flood did not take our boys. The boys of Portsmouth still remain with us, and what a noble lot of boys they are!

"It was the Boy Scouts of the East End, when the flood was rising, that were carrying the household goods of those who were too poor to hire conveyances, and putting them in places of safety.

"If you visited the West End you found the

Scouts there . . . They were clearing away debris, helping to prepare hospitals for the sick. Wherever you went, where lives were being saved, you found Boy Scouts.

"From morning to night these heroes were laboring to save the sufferers of Portsmouth."

Across the country wherever disasters occurred, Boy Scouts turned up to help. Years later this would seem natural enough, but in the early days of Scouting it came as a surprise to Americans. In 1914 a great fire swept the city of Salem, Massachusetts, and the Scouts of Salem worked heroically to help the victims. In 1916 the town of South Amboy, New Jersey, was almost destroyed by an explosion, and its boys labored for days on end. In 1921 a hurricane struck Florida, and Boy Scouts were among the first to do rescue work.

Newspapers wrote glowing stories about the heroism of Boy Scouts. And because Scouting was still new, some people began to think of it as a movement to teach boys to be heroes.

The men behind the Boy Scout movement knew better. They knew it was far more important to help all boys grow into honorable, self-reliant manhood than to create a few heroes. But they also understood that when a boy did a heroic act, it was right that he should receive some kind of award. So in the very early days of Scouting, the National Court of Honor was established to award medals and certificates for heroism.

These awards could go not only to boys but also to Scoutmasters. One of the most heroic —and tragic—stories in the history of Scouting is about a Tennessee Scoutmaster named Jim Wright.

Jim Wright had taken a group of about 20 Scouts out for a weekend hike. One night they were camped in a small cottage near a stream. This stream had not overflowed in a hundred years. But now, in the middle of the night, a flash flood struck.

When Scoutmaster Jim Wright awoke, water was already inches deep on the cabin floor.

Grabbing his flashlight, he went quickly outside. Here the water was several feet deep, so swift he could scarcely stand, and rising rapidly.

Jim knew that if his boys became frightened and tried to run or swim to safety, they would all be drowned. He went quietly back into the cottage and awoke the boys.

"Here is an adventure we didn't expect," he said. "But let's make believe that it was something we had planned all along. The game is to climb on the roof, one at a time. The smallest boys go first."

Joking with his boys, making sure there was no panic, Jim got all of them on the roof. Then he climbed up himself. By now the water was almost knee-deep across the porch.

Soon the cabin itself began to rock. Jim told the boys to take off their shoes, lie down, and hold on. Some of them began to whimper with fear, but Jim told jokes until laughter replaced the whimpers. "I'd be more comfortable at home in bed," he told them. "But then

I wouldn't have nearly as much fresh air."

Upstream from the cabin a bridge washed out. A great wall of water and debris hurtled down the river. It hit the cabin, lifted it, and sent it spinning away. "Hold tight!" Jim shouted. "Just pretend it's a bucking horse and we'll ride it out!"

As the cabin whirled downstream, logs and trees smashed into it. Finally the cabin itself began to break apart. One of the boys was washed away. Instantly Jim Wright leaped after him. In the dark and rushing water, neither Jim nor the boy was seen again.

Before the long night was over and the wrecked cabin washed ashore, seven boys as well as Jim Wright were drowned. But had it not been for the Scoutmaster's heroism, the whole group would almost certainly have died.

Later the National Court of Honor awarded four gold Honor Medals—the highest awards in Scouting—for heroism on that night. One of these went posthumously to Scoutmaster Jim, who had given his life for his boys.

Every year the National Court of Honor meets to consider heroic deeds performed by Scouts all through the country. Almost every issue of *Boys' Life*, the Scouting magazine, tells the story of some Scout who has won an award for heroism.

These Medal of Honor winners are rewarded by the warm thanks of a boy they rescued.

7. The Longest Hikes

From the very first, hiking has been an important part of the Boy Scout program. Probably the two longest hikes in the history of Scouting were those made by Augusto Flores and Paul Siple.

In 1926 Augusto Flores was a sixteen-year-old Peruvian Scout attending school in Buenos Aires, Argentina. With four other Scouts, he began to talk about hiking from Buenos Aires to New York City. This is a distance of more than 10,000 miles, across roadless mountains and unmapped jungles.

At first no one took the idea seriously. A local newspaper wrote: "Five young lunatics are going to try to walk from Buenos Aires to New York City. They are just young boys who probably think the moon is made of green cheese."

On the morning of July 11, 1926, Augusto and his friends set out. Each boy carried an extra shirt, pair of trousers, shoes, socks, underwear, and toilet articles. They had one tent among them. They also had two dogs they had trained to carry the tent. They expected to buy food along the way.

On the first day the boys were so excited they not only walked all day but kept going after dark. When finally they made camp, their pedometers showed they had walked 40 miles. Next morning they were so sore and tired they could hardly walk at all. After that they learned to take things more easily.

Traveling 20 to 30 miles a day, the boys crossed northern Argentina into Bolivia. Now they were in wild mountain country.

It was here that tragedy struck for the first time. They came on a mountain stream that had overflowed its banks. There was no bridge. Elias Torres, the best swimmer of the lot, volunteered to try crossing first. "Maybe it isn't really deep," he said, "and the rest of you can wade across."

The water was very fast and icy cold. It boiled around Elias' knees, then his waist, while the other boys watched from the bank. Suddenly the current swept Elias off his feet. An instant later he vanished beneath the surface.

Augusto Flores and the others raced along the bank. They kept calling Elias' name. For several days they searched up and down the stream, but they never saw their friend again. Sorrowfully they turned back to the nearest village and from there found another way across the river.

The boys made their way slowly over mountains so high it was difficult to breathe. Scrambling toward a bridge, Julio Quinonez was

caught in a landslide and badly injured. The
other boys made a stretcher out of their jack-
ets and two tree limbs. They carried Julio to
the nearest doctor. After resting for two
weeks, he was able to continue.

Then the boys were arrested as spies and
held in prison for several days. Later one of
their dogs was killed by a shepherd who
thought the dog was about to attack his sheep.
The other dog became sick and died.

In Peru the boys got lost in a desert. Without water, exhausted by the terrible heat, they

were barely able to walk. Finally they met a man riding a horse. The boys had the idea he was an outlaw of some kind, running from the law. But he gave them water and told them how to reach the nearest town.

They had been walking for fourteen months and were in the wild jungles of Ecuador when tragedy came again. Nineteen-year-old Manuel Rivera was bitten by a snake and died. Miles from civilization, surrounded by jungle, there was nothing the boys could do except bury their friend and mark his grave with a cross.

Soon after this both Julio and Juan Viletta became sick. For a while they tried to hike on, but in the town of Cali, Ecuador, both had to enter the hospital. The doctor said it would be months before they were well; even then they could not continue the hike.

Only Augusto Flores was left. In a book about his experiences, he wrote later that he had thought of giving up and taking a ship back to his home in Peru. But something made him decide to keep going.

"I had a feeling that I was on my oath as a Scout to finish what I had begun," he wrote. "I didn't go on in a foolish spirit of bravado. I just felt I must."

So on he went, alone now, across Colombia into Panama. There he was met and entertained by Boy Scouts. Soon he was hiking again, through the mountainous jungles of Central America.

In Nicaragua Augusto walked into a revolution. He was captured by the rebels, blindfolded, and then taken to their headquarters. After the rebel chief talked with Augusto, he ordered him released.

In Mexico Augusto was robbed by bandits, who left him without any money. He had nothing but the clothes he was wearing. But he made more money by giving lectures about his experiences.

In May, 1928, Augusto crossed the Mexican border into the United States. Now he rejoiced, for his long hike was nearly over. He had only 2,000 more miles to go! In almost

every town Boy Scouts met him and walked with him. He had good beds to sleep in and good food to eat.

On November 5, 1928, almost two and a half years after he had left Buenos Aires, he walked off a ferryboat from New Jersey into New York City. The long, long hike was over.

Paul Siple's hike was not really all walking, as Augusto's had been, but it was even longer.

While Augusto Flores was plodding through the mountains of South America in 1927, Commander Richard Byrd of the U. S. Navy was preparing an expedition to the South Pole. Commander Byrd had great faith in Scouting. He believed it helped develop boys into the kind of men needed to explore the far reaches of the world. And so he announced that he would take one Boy Scout with him on his trip to the Pole.

Thousands of boys applied. It was Paul Siple, an Eagle Scout from Erie, Pennsylvania, whom Commander Byrd selected.

The expedition set out in 1928 on a big, old-fashioned sailing vessel named the *City of New York*. Paul had been a Sea Scout on Lake Erie, but he knew nothing about a ship like this one. Yet before long Commander Byrd could say: "Paul Siple took up his work in the expedition as a man among men. He stood regular deck watches on shipboard and turned himself into an able-bodied seaman on a full-rigged sailing vessel."

The *City of New York* sailed slowly down the Atlantic Ocean, across the Caribbean Sea, and into the Panama Canal. Here Paul met some of the same Scouts who had met Augusto Flores when he walked across Panama a few months before.

From Panama the ship's course lay southwest across the Pacific to Tahiti, one of the most beautiful islands in the world. After a few days there, the expedition set sail once more, still heading south and west, toward New Zealand. Now the vessel was in what sailors call the "Roaring Forties." These are the waters between the 40th and 50th degrees

Paul Siple, wearing his Arctic gear, en route to Antarctica with the Byrd Expedition

of southern latitude, famous—or infamous—
for the fierce storms that sweep across them.
And here a great storm struck the ship.

Asleep in his bunk, Paul was awakened by
water pouring through the deck overhead and
onto his face. When he stood up, the rolling
of the ship hurled him first to one side, then
the other. Somewhere overhead a man was
shouting, "All hands on deck!"

Half running, half crawling, Paul climbed
the stairway. As he stepped on deck, a huge
wave broke over the ship's bow. It knocked
Paul down and swept him across the deck.
Just in time he clutched the rail. He clung to
it while he fought his way against the wind
to the shelter of the galley.

"Get aloft!" the mate shouted at him. "Help
make the upper topsail fast!"

Into the rigging Paul clambered, along with
other members of the crew. Below them the
ship reeled with the battering of the waves.
Paul would be hanging far out over the water
on one side, then would be swept in a great

arc over the ship and far to the other side. But somehow the sail was made fast.

Eventually the storm blew itself out. A few days later the beautiful, snow-topped mountains of southern New Zealand came into view.

From New Zealand the *City of New York* headed straight for the South Pole. It was now December, the beginning of summer in the Antarctic. Instead of appearing to travel from east to west, the sun now seemed to swing in a slow circle around the horizon. At midnight there were still traces of twilight; by two or three in the morning, sunrise would start. Icebergs began to appear.

Finally there seemed to be nothing but solid ice ahead of the ship. A motor whaling ship, the *Larsen*, joined the *City of New York* and took her in tow. The *Larsen* would crunch her way through the ice; the ice would close in behind her; then the old sailing ship at the end of her cable would smash into the ice. Paul felt certain the sides of the ship would cave in, but it kept going.

This ice gave way for a while to open water, and once more the *City of New York* moved under her own sail. But not for long. One day Paul heard the lookout shout, "Barrier ahead!" Everyone dashed on deck.

Ahead of them was a great, white, shimmering wall across the sea. As the ship drew nearer, the wall seemed to rise higher and higher. This was the Ross Barrier—a solid wall of ice towering 100 feet or more into the air!

The *City of New York* was made fast alongside the Barrier, and the supplies were unloaded. Then by dog sled and tractor, the men of Commander Byrd's expedition went inland to set up a base they called Little America. The empty ship turned back for New Zealand.

Although Paul was the youngest member of the party, he had done a man's work from the first. Now in the Antarctic he was given a dog sled to drive. Along with other members of the expedition, he made exploratory trips of 50 miles or more, sometimes riding on the sled, sometimes running beside his dogs. Nights were spent in a sleeping bag in the snow beneath a tiny, one-man tent.

It was on a comparatively short trip that Paul had his closest brush with death. Winter had begun to close in while some of the expedition's supplies were still stacked along the Barrier. If the supplies were not moved quickly, they would be buried under new snow and lost forever. So Paul and two other drivers set out for the Barrier, five miles from the camp.

The day was bitterly cold. Wind whipped snow off the ice and blew it in their faces. As Paul and the men traveled, the velocity of the wind increased. By the time they reached the Barrier, it was blowing 50 miles an hour and driving fresh snow in front of it. Nearly blinded, Paul and his friends loaded their sleds as quickly as possible and started back for camp.

Now the wind was blowing with almost hurricane force. In single file the three dog teams moved along the trail, Paul's team bringing up the rear. Because the men had gained experience from previous storms, they had placed orange flags every 100 yards along the route. But now the blinding snow made it impossible to see from one flag to the next. The wind, coming at right angles, forced the dogs off the trail. The drivers had to fight to get them back. Worse yet, the trail itself was disappearing under the snow.

Suddenly Paul realized that for several minutes he had been walking with his face turned down against his coat to protect it from the wind. When he looked up, he could no longer see the men with their dog teams in front of him. He could see nothing except the driving snow. And the snow under his feet was soft, not packed hard as it would have been on the trail. He was off the trail and had lost his way!

For a few moments he stood still, fighting down panic. In these conditions fear could be as deadly as the cold. He forced himself to think clearly. He realized that he and his dog team must have drifted in the direction the wind was blowing. Therefore the trail would be somewhere in the opposite direction, against the wind, and he should follow his tracks back to it.

He turned his dog team, but the dogs did not want to pull the sled into the bitter wind. He had to take the lead dog by the collar and force it to move. Before he had gone five

yards, the tracks he had made coming here were covered by new snow.

Now he had nothing but the wind itself to guide him. Struggling to stay upright and keep the dogs moving, he fought his way into the storm. He could scarcely see the snow beneath his feet. But all at once he realized it was more firm than it had been. He was recrossing the trail!

Once more he changed direction. In a short distance he found one of the orange flags. In another 100 yards he came on the other dog teams, their drivers anxiously waiting for him. Battling the storm, they made their way back to camp.

All that long winter Paul Siple and the other men lived in houses completely covered by snow. When they wanted to go from one house to another, they moved through tunnels. By the light of lanterns, Paul helped with the scientific study of penguins and seals. When summer returned, he once more drove his dog team on long explorations. And as winter began to close in again, ships came to take the party home.

Some years later Dr. Paul Siple would make another trip to the Antarctic, this time as a recognized scientist. In World War II and again in the Korean War he would be an adviser to the army on how to live and fight in extreme cold, helping others with the knowledge he had first gained as a Boy Scout.

On a later trip in 1947, Dr. Siple brought back a crabeater seal as a hunting trophy.

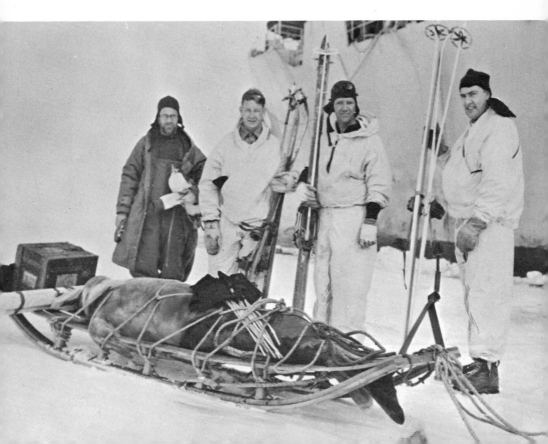

8. To Keep America Bright

The canoe moved slowly, the three men
barely working at their paddles as they gazed
around them. The river was dark, almost
coffee-colored, flowing between walls of moss-
hung oaks. On the banks the trees grew upright, but in the water they seemed to grow
upside down, their limbs reaching toward a
blue, underwater sky.

"It's beautiful," Explorer Jim Kendrick said.
"But we haven't seen much wildlife."

"Almost no fish. Few big ones anyway," Jimmy Keene said.

Advisor Mitchell Hope nodded. "A few years ago," he said, "you wouldn't have seen any. In fact, we couldn't even have been here."

He referred to a time when the river had been covered by a white scum from bank to bank. The scum was the result of sludge dumped into the river by phosphate plants upstream. It had killed the fish. It had killed the underwater grasses. It had even killed some of the plants along the banks. It had changed Florida's Peace River, one of the most beautiful streams in America, into a foul-smelling River of Death.

After conservationists finally forced the phosphate companies to stop polluting the river, the water had slowly begun to clear. Once more the underwater grasses began to grow. The streams were restocked with fingerling bass and bream.

Now in the fall of 1962, the river had recovered enough natural beauty for the Scouts

of Explorer Post 410 of Wauchula, Florida, to plan a weekend canoe trip along it. Explorers Jim Kendrick and Jimmy Keene with Advisor Mitchell Hope were scouting ahead for camp sites.

"A few more years and the river will be almost as beautiful as ever," Hope said. And added, "*If* we can keep it from being polluted again. But that's a battle that has to go on forever."

While he spoke, the canoe rounded a bend

in the river. Here the bank had been eroded by past floods. "Look!" Jimmy Keene said suddenly. "What's that?"

Something large and white stuck out of the mud bank. "It looks like a bone," Mitchell Hope said. "A fossil of some kind."

The boys nosed the canoe into the bank. Then, working carefully with their bare hands and pocket knives, they dug up the bone. It was obviously a jawbone, but bigger than any jawbone any of them had seen or heard of.

Beneath it they could see still other bones.

"I think we have found something important," Hope said. "And I think we had better get some real experts to advise us."

Next day a telephone call to the Florida State Museum brought a paleontologist. He identified the fossil as part of a mastodon ("Old Masty," the Explorers called it), a prehistoric ancestor of present-day elephants. Some of the other bones found near it were of even older and stranger animals.

So it was that Explorer Post 410 began one of the most exciting conservation projects ever tackled by Boy Scouts. Experts from both the Florida State Museum and the Smithsonian Institution in Washington joined in the work. They helped the boys and taught them at the same time. The longer the project went on, the bigger it got, and the more exciting.

"Digging for fossils is like hunting for buried treasure," one Explorer said. "Except here we really find it. We never know what we are going to find, but it is always exciting."

80

One important find was the fossil of an imperial mammoth with tusks nine feet long. It was one of the finest mammoth fossils ever found in America. But even more important was the discovery of one small tooth. Experts identified it as having belonged to a pronghorn antelope, thought to have lived 10 million years ago, and probably the only fossil of this species ever found!

Some of the fossils discovered have been given to the Florida State Museum. Some have gone to the Smithsonian Institution. But many have stayed with Post 410. In fact, the people of Wauchula, Florida got so excited over their boys' work, they built a museum to house it.

And at least two of the boys whose interest was sparked by helping dig up the skeleton of Old Masty are now building their careers in paleontology.

The conservation of America's natural resources, of wildlife, of wilderness, and of the natural beauty of the countryside, has always been a primary objective of Scouting. Not all the work has been as dramatic as the recovery of 10-million-year-old bones, but it has been of tremendous value to the nation.

A historian once said that the natural beauty of America was not destroyed as much by vandalism and industry as by neglect. A Scout patrol picking up bottle caps and beer cans around a roadside picnic table can improve the looks of a small area. Five thousand patrols doing small jobs can improve the looks of the country.

The improvement may not always be instantaneous. Scouts sometimes need to take a long view. But one of the aims of Scouting is to help a boy understand his American heritage and want to preserve it for boys who follow.

About 20 years ago the Scouts of Michigan City, Indiana, set out to improve some land they wanted to use as a camp site. It was barren dune country with only clumps of scrubby trees here and there. The boys planted pine trees. They did a lot of tiring work under a burning sun. The little trees didn't look like much when they were planted, but the boys kept at it. The next year they went back and planted more. And the year after.

This New Jersey Boy Scout plants a tree for future Scouts to enjoy.

Now if you visit Camp To-Pe-Ne-Bee, you will find what looks like virgin forest. Tall trees throw a thick shade on needle-covered ground. Wildlife has returned. And today's Scouts have a far finer camp ground than would have been possible without those Scouts of 20 years ago.

Since the beginning of Scouting, one American President after another has recognized the important contributions Scouts can make to national conservation. In World War I President Woodrow Wilson asked the Scouts to locate and number all the black walnut trees in the country. It was a tremendous undertaking, but black walnut was needed for the propellers of those primitive World War I airplanes, and only certain trees could be cut. Before the end of the war, Scouts had located and marked what would have amounted to 5,200 train carloads of black walnut timber.

After World War II the Sea Explorers of Ship 25, Ithaca, New York, planted the millionth tree in a project that had begun 20 years before. The tree, a white spruce, was dedicated to six former Ithaca Sea Explorers who had been killed in the war.

In 1965 President Lyndon Johnson challenged the Scouts to take part in a drive to keep America beautiful. From coast to coast the boys responded. In one year almost 5,000 Scouts in Buffalo, New York, earned conservation certificates for work in tree planting and erosion control.

Near Salt Lake City, Scouts turned 32 acres of burned-over wasteland into winter range for mule deer by planting bitter brush. In Topeka, Kansas, Scouts spent 25,000 hours building a park that had been destroyed by a tornado.

Joseph Brunton, Chief Scout Executive of the United States, wrote in *Boys' Life* that it is the duty of Scouts to "keep our America bright 'from sea to shining sea.'"

It is a duty the Scouts are not neglecting.

9. Jamborees

Sir Baden-Powell liked the word "Jamboree." He didn't know just where he had heard it first, and he wasn't sure exactly what it meant, but he liked the sound.

In the very early days of Scouting, British Scouts had held "rallies" and "exhibitions." But B-P didn't like the sound of these two words.

"The next time Scouts have a big get-together," he told a friend, "we'll call it a Jamboree."

His friend had never heard the word, so he looked it up in a dictionary. "Now wait a minute," he told B-P. "You can't call a Boy Scout meeting a Jamboree. It just won't do."

"Why not?" B-P asked.

"Well," his friend said, "the word means: 'A carousal; a noisy drinking bout; a spree; hence any noisy merrymaking.'"

B-P laughed. "That's all right. When a gang of Scouts gets together, it ought to be a noisy merrymaking. And I think we can forget about the first part of the definition."

(As it turned out, B-P's decision was important not only to Scouting, but to the English language. Now if you look up the word in a new dictionary, you will still find the old meaning, but you will also find that it means: "A large gathering of members of the Boy Scouts, usually national or international in scope.")

B-P planned for the first International Jamboree to be held in England in 1915. However, the outbreak of World War I in 1914 put an end to those plans. It was not until 1920, when the war was over, that the first Jamboree could be held.

The first Jamboree was held in a huge, glass-roofed exhibition hall in London—the only International Jamboree to be held indoors. Six thousand Scouts from many nations attended. One thousand of them lived in the auditorium itself; the other 5,000 pitched tents in a park and rode to and from the auditorium by bus or train.

The last night of this Jamboree reached a climax that no Scout who was there will ever forget. B-P was in the Royal Box together with the Chief Scouts from the other countries. The Scouts themselves were massed on the floor of the auditorium. The flags of all their nations floated over them. Scouts from one country after another came forward to put on their brief final exhibitions. As the Jamboree was ending, Sir Baden-Powell arose to make the farewell speech.

Then something happened that the boys had

prepared among themselves. B-P knew nothing about it. Before he could begin his speech, one of the Scouts cried out in a loud, clear voice: "We, the Scouts of the World, salute you, Sir Robert Baden-Powell—Chief Scout of the World!"

Together the standard bearers of all the nations dipped their flags in B-P's honor. There was a moment's hush. Then the roaring cheers of the boys shook the building.

For some time Sir Baden-Powell stood motionless. Nothing in his honor-filled life had moved him so deeply. At last he raised his hand in the Scout sign. Instantly the cheering stopped. An almost electric silence filled the great hall.

Sir Baden-Powell's voice was tight with emotion. "Brother Scouts," he said, "I ask you to make a solemn choice. Differences exist between the peoples of the world in thought and sentiment, just as they do in language and physique. The war has taught us that if one nation tries to impose its particular will upon

Scouts from different parts of the world get to know each other better at Jamborees.

others, cruel reaction is bound to follow. The Jamboree has taught us that if we exercise mutual forbearance and give-and-take, then there is sympathy and harmony. If it be your will, let us go forth from here determined that we will develop among ourselves and our boys that comradeship, through the worldwide spirit of the Scout brotherhood, so that we may help to develop peace and happiness in the world and good will among men. Brother Scouts, answer me—will you join me in this endeavor?"

With a roar the Scouts answered, "Yes!"

This idea of worldwide friendship and Scout brotherhood has been the basic theme of every International Jamboree since then—in Denmark in 1924, England in 1929, Hungary in 1933, Holland in 1937, France in 1947, Austria in 1951, Canada in 1955, England in 1957, the Philippines in 1959, Greece in 1963, and for the first time in the United States in 1967.

The 1967 Jamboree was held in Farragut State Park near Coeur d'Alene, Idaho. The camp ground was a grassy plain beside a huge lake. All around it wooded mountains rose against the sky. Here were gathered more than 13,000 Scouts from almost 100 countries.

The boys lived in tents, two boys in each tent. Several tents of boys from one area made up a patrol. The patrols were grouped in sub-camps. And each sub-camp had boys from many countries. In this way boys from Florida not only met boys from Ohio and Oregon and California, they also met boys from Australia, India, Japan and other countries. To the American Scouts it was a great surprise

Scouts link arms as they spell FRIENDSHIP in the Wide Game at the 1967 Jamboree.

to find how many of the visitors could speak English. If they couldn't speak English, it made little difference. The boys still carried on conversations in a kind of sign language mixed with roars of laughter.

The most popular game at the Jamboree was designed to carry out the theme of international friendship. It was called the Wide Game. Each boy was given one letter: F, R, I, E, N, D, S, H, I, or P. Then he had to find boys from other countries who had the other letters necessary to spell out FRIENDSHIP. This newly-formed group, sometimes speaking ten different languages, had to put on a stunt together. They might build a pyramid or stage an Indian dance or sing a song they had made up.

Flag raising was an event that took place every morning. It was a sight no boy there would ever forget. In a great arc around the main campground were tall flag poles, one for each country at the Jamboree. In front of each sub-camp was a short, double row of flag poles for Scout flags and pennants. Also, each patrol had a pole for its own national flag.

At 8:20 each morning a cannon boomed. Quickly the boys lined up. There were two Scouts at each flag pole. The other Scouts stood in formation behind them throughout the great camp. A second cannon boomed. While the Scouts saluted, standing stiffly at attention, a thousand flags rippled upward against the morning sky.

Lady Baden-Powell, B-P's widow, was a

guest of honor at the Jamboree. Deeply moved, she watched as the flags of a hundred countries rose over the camp. Nothing could show better the tremendous growth of the work her husband had helped to start.

Another kind of International Scout Jamboree is held every year—a Jamboree at which all the Scouts stay home, yet visit with one another all over the world. This is the Jamboree-On-The-Air for ham radio operators. On a certain day each year, the Jamboree begins

Lady Baden-Powell greets a young Scout from Kenya at the Twelfth World Jamboree.

at 0001, G.M.T. (one minute after midnight, Greenwich Meridian Time) and lasts until 2359 (one minute before the next midnight) G.M.T. Scouts who are ham operators call "CQ Jamboree" by either voice or code and talk with one another around the world.

Not all Jamborees, of course, are international. Scouts in almost every country have Jamborees of their own. In the United States, Jamborees have been held in Washington, D.C., California, Colorado, and at Valley Forge, Pennsylvania. It was at Valley Forge that President Lyndon Johnson reminded the Scouts, as Sir Baden-Powell had done many years before, of the meaning of Scout Brotherhood.

"The American idea," the President said, "is, first of all, the belief in freedom and the rights of man. Government was to be chosen and directed by the people. And every individual citizen was to have the right to speak his views, worship as he wanted, and be safe from arbitrary acts of government. . . . This dedication to freedom was founded on the great moral truth that all men are created equal. This was a recognition that all men were created equal in the eyes of God. Being equal, the poorest and most oppressed among us had the same right as all others to share in government, enjoy liberty, and pursue happiness as far as his abilities would take him. It is up to you to carry this idea forward. For it is not yet a reality in all this land. . . .

"The qualities you will require for this task," the President said, "are those contained in the Boy Scout Oath. Its pledge has a meaning not only for you, but for all our citizens. What that pledge means is the theme of this Jamboree."

It is, in fact, the serious meaning which lies behind the fun of every Boy Scout Jamboree. But more than that. It is the spirit that has made Scouting grow into a world-wide movement. It is the spirit that will keep it growing for years to come.